IN LIGHT OF WISDOM

Swami Amar Jyoti

Truth Consciousness
Boulder, Colorado

Other books by the same Author:

Retreat Into Eternity: *an Upanishad – book of aphorisms*
Spirit of Himalaya: *the story of a Truth seeker*

About the Author:

Satsang Notes of Swami Amar Jyoti

Book design by the Author

Printed on fine quality paper and
handbound in Boulder, Colorado

Copyright © 1983 by Swami Amar Jyoti
all rights reserved

First Edition (Limited) 1983
Second Edition 1984

acknowledgements:
editing assistance: S. Stuhlmiller
graphics, layout: Ronnye Russell

Published by: Truth Consciousness
　　　　　　　Gold Hill, Salina Star Route
　　　　　　　Boulder, Colorado 80302
　　　　　　　(303) 447-1637

Library of Congress Catalog Card Number: 84-50889
Title: In Light of Wisdom
　　　by Swami Amar Jyoti

ISBN 0-933572-05-0

Contents

Truth	7
Ego	15
Conceptions	20
Understanding	39
God	48
Love	53
Being	61

'Like a rushing river from the mountains' God pours forth His light-full wisdom. He speaks to us in every morning's dawn, every dark night; everything is Him speaking. But knowing that we hardly hear Him, much less catch and hold on to what He says, He speaks to us also in the ways that we speak, in languages old and new. Always He has spoken to us, through saints and seers, sages and prophets, in all places and ages. There is something very special about their language, something 'crisp, crystal clear.' It lights up our minds like dazzling lightning in the night sky, it warms and opens our hearts like the sudden springtime; it is compelling and undeniable. We somehow know that it is Truth. In instant recognition, in relief and gratitude, we embrace it immediately, and though we may again turn our backs on it for eons, it never leaves us; as soon as we turn around it is totally there, fitting, perfect, ours from the beginning of all time.

So like a rushing river from the mountains, crisp and crystal clear, joyful, sparkling, lovely, utterly generous, cleansing, spontaneous, free, simple, very powerful, deep and true, come the Satsangs*of Swami Amar Jyoti from which the poems in this book have been selected. Swamiji's Satsangs are pervaded by His love and wisdom; they are the Truth after which we thirst, the beacon of rescue for which we watch, the liberation for which we aspire.

Often Master humbly apologizes for His 'poor English' (it is not His mother tongue) but His devotees smile because His language has a quality which takes the breath away. It is a majestic, joyful and truly poetic language. These are a few, a very few, of the spontaneous poems gathered from His utterances, in which He crystallizes His message. They blaze forth to illuminate, to reveal, in beauty of form and clarity of meaning, the Light of His Wisdom.

Wisdom which one could hardly glean from volumes is as if focused in these poems into a brilliant point we can instantly see. There is a perfect blending in them of loving tenderness and lofty power, of beauty and knowledge, that expresses and conveys Master's own nature. Gems of purity, freely bestowed, in that special language that enters into us and brings forth a response from within us that may amaze and delight us as much as do the poems themselves. There is an intimacy of communication in them that we all crave and search for. Master speaks not only to our hearts but from our heart of hearts and we are blessed to hear the language of our Soul.

Communion with the Truth through the Master's presence and word

*This whole
universe is
God's dream only.*

Truth

That's the nature of the bird
of the soul;
the soul has wings
but it has forgotten
it's in a cage.
It tries, it sees
that the cage is there,
but it gets habituated,
thinks the cage
is home.

If it were the real home
it would be giving him joy
peace and freedom.
But his eyes are always out
beyond, somewhere,
knowingly or unknowingly,
seeking That.

If ever he would remember
his true Goal,
sincerely, truly,
then he could not remain
in the cage . . .

Are you feeling
you are in a cage?
Are you feeling
you are in bondage?
Not by saying,
but by inner feelings,
that you are in ignorance?
Or have you forgotten
where the walls are?

Let us not confuse
furrows of the mind
those ruts
with the path.
The way is so broad
like the sky
that has no boundaries.
In that Cosmic Consciousness
you'll be joyful
always
full with Light.

You'll wonder
why at all
you retained all those cobwebs:
to decorate
the spider's web
of your mind?

Your path
you have to find
through you
but
don't get stuck
in the dead end
of your own mind.

The path
is that which opens
into the unlimited
vista of release
far beyond duality
into boundless Consciousness.

'Truth shall make you free.'
That's crisp, crystal clear.
It can survive any argument,
any discussion, or debate.
Truth can stand any challenges,
not by its own determination
but by its own proven victory;
not by what I say or you say,
but by Itself, Truth shines.
It shall prevail.

We want our dreams to come true
but
is the value in dreams
or Truth?
What if we were seeing only Truth?
In Its light
All dreams would be
fictitious conceptions
wishful thinkings or notions
or cherished pet ideals.

Howsoever philosophically we may explain
it won't satisfy us
unless we come to Truth,
back to the Source.

In one spark of fire
there is the whole fire
it can ignite
whole cities and nations
one spark!

That's how the Truth
of one Person
from age to age
can shake the whole earth.

If you want peace
            be peaceful
if you want joy
            be joyful
if you don't want anybody to hurt you
            be harmless
if you want everything to happen
    as you wish
            be truthful!
(unless, by the time you become truthful,
your wishes may change!)

Ego

Nobody is blocking your path
 except you.
If there is any devil on earth
ultimately
when you find him
it'll be *you*.

It's not the Cosmos
that's going to tumble down
back into your bottleneck,
into the bottle;
it's the breath in the bottle
which has to mingle
with the Cosmic breath.

It's the Oneness
which the objective world
has to seek
rather than expecting
the subjective Divine to descend
into
egotistical bottles
with labels on them.

If you quietly enter your heart
you'll see this:
that when you said
'i didn't know' or
'i didn't understand'
you were trying to cover up
willfully.

When we avoid seeing minutely
judging ourselves on the surface only
we say 'i don't know, i don't know'
all the while,
underneath pressing a certain point.
That's called diplomacy.
How can it give us peace?

Live for the ego,
incur miseries.
Live for God,
be free
a blissful soul.

We want peace and happiness
on the basis of time and space.
Time creates history,
space creates geography.
Within the dimensions
of history and geography
we create philosophy
and within the domain of philosophy,
techniques,
and within the scope of techniques,
denominations,
and denominations create battles and wars
with the ultimate results being
no peace and no happiness.

Conceptions

You are fighting
with yourself.
You have to resolve it,
not fight with it.
Resolve it
resolve
dissolve
solve.

It takes no time
to open to Him
if you care.
It has to be
both ways,
mutual.

You cannot clap
with one hand
except on your
own cheek.

Not pride
not boasting
not self-assertion
nor insistence
nor imposition
but courage
coupled with
inner letting-go;
then you shall be free
and *everything* else
shall be added unto you
because you have
the highest wealth,
Light
within you.

It's not self-image
which shall make you free,
please not!
Don't make God great
because you want to be great;
you'll lose both.

Frustration
is the result
of wrong seeking.
Wrong seeking produces
wrong efforts
wrong efforts produce
excuses
excuses produce
more bondage
and more bondage proves
more miserable
more miseries make you
more negative
more negativities make you
disappointed
suicidal
and what not.

This is how
the circle goes round
and round.

Desire excites.
Excitement may
sometimes
elevate us
but
will depress us
eventually.
Inspiration elevates
further
and further.

Avoid the holocaust of contrast.
And what are you contrasting
or comparing?
One side with the other,
both sides when created
by the same Creator,
both sides of the coin
made by the same mint.

See the Thing in Itself.

Somewhere
in you
you know (the Truth)
and when you
stubbornly
insist that
you don't know
then you
go up
and down.

This is witnessing:
stand apart
from your mind
in the space,
lift up your mind
with the leverage
of your will.

After you have rejected
what was to be rejected
and accepted
what was to be accepted,
then
only acceptance
remains hollow.

At that end you'll say,
'What's this acceptance for, even?
i don't need it.'
Then
you'll arrive at
'Who am I?'

It's dangerous
to be something;
it's foolish
to be nothing;
it's wise
to be everything.

When someone calls you
stupid and foolish
you mind it.
Knowing this,
the Sages use the word
'ignorance.'

Ignorance is something
you don't know
and when you are thinking
about what you don't know,
what are you going
to get from it?

'Oh, i'm thinking
in order to know it,'
but the whole fallacy is
because you're thinking
you're not knowing it;
you're blocking it.

Stop thinking
and start *seeing;*
then you'll know it.

It's a fallacy
of our intellect
to formulate
the Impersonal
and the formless;
it's a habit, simply.

Whatever is pervading
Impersonal,
what is intrinsically
Essential
(we again put
in words
and formulations).
There we miss the point.

The time you are trying
to explain It,
trying to
understand It,
is the very time
you are missing It.

Truth itself
the Bliss
the Kingdom of God within you
is a universal fact.
It's not a Christian
Hindu or Buddhist doctrine.

When you utter the same fact
in Sanskrit
                it is Hinduism
in Pali
                it is Buddhism
and in English
                it's Christianity.

It's the same Thing we are talking about:
Spirit
Light
Consciousness
Bliss
Kingdom of God.

Where else
will Light shine
except where there is
darkness?
Where else will you seek
redress?

When the mind is confused
and in misery,
seeking peace
is the solution.
But you are brooding
upon confusions;
you are brooding
upon darkness.

Human psychology
has its own illusory domain
and there you have to
experience
experience within experience,
darkness rolling
within darkness,
illusion building up
illusion.

All the fictitious
statistics follow,
measurement,
quantitatively
all illusion.
Qualitatively,
it's the same Thing.

Achieving That
how are you going to lose this?
On the contrary
you are getting everything
because this is all
made of That.

You, me, the world,
whole galaxies
everything
is made of that Truth
that Light
Consciousness
God.

How then
by achieving That
are you being impractical?
Can you logically
even disprove it?
What to say
of experiencing
It!

If there are any miseries
and frictions and struggles
there's really only one:
because you are putting limits
between you and That
you and others
you and all.

These limitations
are causing miseries
because they ignore
the Reality of Oneness.

When you are
there
this is
here
when you are
here
That is
there.

It's sheer illusion
to try to separate
the phenomena
from the Reality,
and then try
to love phenomena first.
It just doesn't happen that way.
Naturally
we end in failure.

You don't have to try
to achieve
unity with others.
It is fallacious thinking
and doing.
Realize the unity
of everything
and everyone
within you
first.

Separation is fictitious;
you can separate
only in conception,
not in reality.

And we build theses
upon this separation
trying to bridge across it.
It cannot be bridged
because it is
never separated in the first place
except in your conception.
So remove your conception;
the separation will end.

When you dissolve your conception
things are just as real
as they could be.

Understanding

Satsang is always Satsang
it goes on
to remind us
about what we forget.

There is nothing new,
only it is said in new ways
in a new fashion
so that somewhere
it touches us.

There is nothing to teach
it's always to remind
or awaken
that which you
already have.

Even if you experience
ten million experiences
within darkness,
there is no solution
to darkness
except
to come out of darkness
into Light.

The whole world is like that
can you imagine
that we are all living in a bar,
intoxicated with one
or the other brand?

You tell me:
(you don't have to say yes)
if you have some other answer
I'll be happy to hear that;
are we not intoxicated
illusory ghosts only?

While you are conceptualizing
you are not conscious.
If you are conscious,
you have no need
to conceptualize.
Simply: It *is*.

Certainly we are living
compared to stones,
but compared to
Spirit
we are dead.

In a dream you think
you are seeing and observing
but those who are standing
outside you, awake,
know you are sleeping still.

The living ones
call the dead 'the dead'
and higher living Beings
call living ones the dead.

Mind is not capable
of knowing everything
fully;
it's always knowing something
which is equal
to knowing nothing.

Partial knowledge
is no knowledge
and any knowledge
devoid of absoluteness
doesn't free us.

Freedom is not
    arrogance
freedom is not
    self-assertion
Freedom is
    where you feel joy.

Without learning anything
you know everything
and having everything
you are bound by nothing;
this is the true nature
of a free soul.

Bliss is within us.
there's no journey about it.
You have to realize it.
How?
Reject the things
which are barriers
and impositions upon Bliss:
the worries of the past
and the plannings
of the future.

If you want true Bliss
forgive and forget
everything, without exception,
any sin, even to the extent of
'Forgive them, Father
for they do not know
what they are doing.'
If you can do that
then only can you hope for Bliss;
not otherwise.

This whole
universe is
God's dream only.

God

Divine the true,
Divine the beautiful,
Divine the good,
Divine the all-pervading,
Divine the most merciful,
most loving;
what deficiencies has It
that we are not mad after It?
What are the disqualifications
of the Divine?
Pity!

Seek
the God you accept,
you recognize.
That God is supreme for you
not for comparison
philosophy
or understanding:
God is
to be loved.

That's how
God *is*
whether you go on
rejecting other Gods
and Prophets
or accepting all
it remains the same fact:
God is God,
God is One.

Those who want
to be spiritual
Divine
liberated
free souls
blissful
have to
just tumble down
their foreheads
at the feet
of their Lord
and say,
God, Thou knowest
everything;
i don't.

Love

Greater the devotion
more the knowledge,
Greater the knowledge,
more the love.

If 'knowledge' does not awaken
more love in you
it's not knowledge;
it's dry intellectualism.

If it's not true devotion
but just mechanical worship,
it will keep you dull.

Cold hearted people
cannot have knowledge
nor can wise people
stop the love
springing
from their hearts.

Love others
because Light is in them
not because of the person.
Otherwise
one day you'll miss them
you'll lose them.

Love others
because Light is within them.
That's the Principle.
Then you'll never miss them
even if they die
because the Principle
is still existent.

Embodied or disembodied
it's the Principle
which fulfills.

Work hard, love your God;
pray, meditate
If you want to be near Him.
But don't tell Him
you want to be special;
He may turn His face away.

He'll pick up
according to His choice,
according to deservingness,
not by demands.
Why should God
follow our advice anyway?

Do grocery
at the grocery shop,
not when you love.
Politics
are somewhere else.
When you love
there can be no politics.
There is no brokerage
in love.
Keep it
free.

Love doesn't claim
     doesn't expect
     doesn't seek revenge
     doesn't grumble and complain
     doesn't find faults.

If any of these things remain
love is not,
and yet we justify
all these things
in the name of love!
That's the tragedy.

As if in the name of love
we fight,
in the name of peace
we kill,
in the name of renunciation
we claim.
It's all the folly
of human nature,
it's frailties, its complexities.

And if everything else fails,
weep;
if weeping doesn't bear fruit,
abuse.
If abuses don't produce anything,
hurl whatever you have in hand:
glasses, stones, vases, books,
like that;
and if that doesn't work
then go and wring the neck
of the person;
if that doesn't pay either
then wrestle him to the ground,
sit on his chest and say
'i love you
don't you know
i love you?!'

You should know
       what price you have to pay.
If you are prepared
       for that price
       then seek Love.
If you are not prepared
       don't take the biplane
       to the moon.

Being

There is a way
beyond the ways
which is not a way . . .

Light is within you
already.
You have gained nothing
lost nothing
you are one with It
already,
just *realize* it.
How?
Let That happen
let this go.
Be One.

The Light
surrounds you
all the time
as a halo.

Everyone
is the embodiment
of Light.
Not only so,
everyone *is*
vibrating Light.

You have to let go
relax
in order to be
That,
what you
already
are.

In the domain
of unconsciousness
you see within and without.
In the pervadedness of Consciousness
there is no within and without;
it's all
It.

Basic truth is
non-denominational
non-dogmatic
universal.
When you go to the core
of the Principle
we all are
One.

Once you
realize
the Absolute,
relativity
is just your
playing cards.

Grow
you can grow to infinity,
contract
you can contract into a ditch.
(Just a hole is enough for a worm.)
And grow
you can be Omnipotent,
you can expand to any limitless
universal space.

Anything in finitude
cripples your freedom.
Infinity is freedom,
and your soul has the capacity
to be infinite.

Forgetting that *Being*
you are lost
into the process
of becoming.
You get tied up
with becoming
something
all the time
you want to be this,
you want to be that.

You don't want to end
the becoming
into Being
wherein lies the whole secret
of becoming.

Becoming is itself not an independent
something
it's a radiation of Being,
it's a projection of Consciousness,
that basic eternal Essence
which Thou art.

The Source supplies you
with the energy
to reach It.

When you seek
the Light
It
shall enlighten
your path.

And when you are longing
for the Divine,
for the Truth,
That shall give you
power and energy
to tread on.

Your center of Being is within you.
If it were not
you would not revolve as a circle.
You can't have a circle
without a center, can you?
No geometry would design that way.

You are escaping that center
and going round and round
the circumference.

The center is at its own place;
the circumference revolves.
You escape the center
because you fear,
if you get into the center
you are lost.
You're not lost!
You're reaching your Source,
the Light of lights,
the unimaginable Something,
indescribable,
your true Essence,
you call God.

You'll emerge as a conscious being
once you touch
that center of Consciousness.

And simple
is the Goal.
Light
Truth
God
your Self,
Spirit.

It's all simple,
indivisible,
the minutest
particle
where there are
no more pions
or gluons
and muons
and electrons;
the last particle
nameless
whatever
It may be
ya, It has
no name
It has no
description either.
It's very
transparent
the Ultimate
Factor
whatever
you call It.

On That
you meditate;
sing the glories
of That.
You'll *know*.

The joy which is
in Revelation
is nowhere else.
No amount of
perception
thinking
projection
planning
doing
efforts
achieving
ever will give you
that joy
that radiance
which Revelation does.

In the center of the circle
is seen the perfect formula of creation
a perfect equation
between Light and phenomena.

Get to the Source first
and open your eyes;
the whole phenomena is Light-full.

You'll see then
there never was darkness.

Stream, know thy Source
ray, know thy Center
man, know thy Self;
that will be
the real solution.